A World City

Birmingham and its people portrayed

A World City Birmingham and its people portrayed

Birmingham
Libraries

Contents

Above *Nick Hedges*, The Copthorne Hotel and Birmingham Central Library *1998*
Previous Page *Tom Merilion*, Richard and Gillian, Moseley Road Baths *1997*

A World City

Christopher Upton

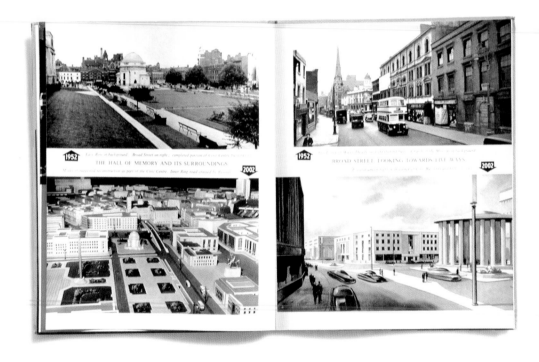

Above *Paul S Cadbury*, Birmingham, Fifty Years On, Bournville Village Trust, published in 1952
Left hand page: The Hall of Memory and its surroundings in 1952 and artist's impression of 2002
Right hand page: Broad Street looking towards Five Ways in 1952 and artist's impression of 2002

I was much surprised at the place, but more at the people. They were a species I had never seen; they possessed a vivacity I had never beheld. I had been among dreamers, but now I saw men awake. William Hutton (1741)

Great cities, they say, never sleep, but they are always dreaming. Some dream solely of their past; some only of their future. Sometimes those dreams wake up blinking on planners' desks under strong white light; others fall asleep again in archives or museum vaults.

Birmingham has been dreaming forwards for over a century, imagining where it wanted to be, shrugging off one skin for another. Joseph Chamberlain's great Improvement Scheme of the 1870s was one of the first, an ambitious and expensive plan to rid the city centre of its slums and replace them with wide boulevards and grand shops. The Victorian high-rise and the terracotta palaces of Corporation Street have been the lasting legacy of this plan. A generation later, William Hayward dreamt of a vast civic square at the bottom of Broad Street, pulling together exhibition halls, libraries and council offices into a vast complex that even Mussolini would have envied. A model of that dream lies in the Museum & Art Gallery; the reality was interrupted and then liquidated by the Second World War. Only Baskerville House and the Hall of Memory give a distant echo of what might have been.

Fifty years ago – in 1952 to be precise – Paul Cadbury published his vision of where he imagined the city of Birmingham would be half a century later. Much of what Cadbury envisaged has indeed come to pass, nationally as well as locally. The corner shop has been largely supplanted by what he called the 'grocerteria'; estates have replaced the back-to-back courts; buildings have grown inexorably upwards, and glass has become the new brick.

Cadbury's optimistic vision seemed to capture the public mood of post-war Britain. The dreams came thick and fast in these years. There was a shared need for something new, something different. What had the war been for, if not for a better world and a brighter Birmingham? In an atmosphere of austerity and rationing, dreams were the one item not in short supply.

But then, unexpectedly and with bewildering speed, the vision became the reality. The planners and the speculators moved in and Birmingham became a huge laboratory of modernism. Within ten years what was once the Victorian open market had become a shopping centre, one of the first in the country and by far the biggest. An urban motorway – another new concept – swept traffic under and around the city centre. The railway station disappeared underground and carried another shopping complex on its back, and the pedestrians disappeared too, into underpasses and subterranean shops, invariably coming up in the wrong place.

There was irresistible change out in the suburbs too. The tunnel-backs and the terraces of Duddeston and Nechells, Summer Lane and Ladywood, were no

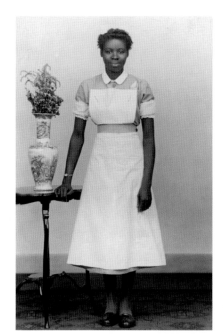

more, replaced by multi-storeys and maisonettes. There were new lamps for old, radiators for ranges, and rubbish disposal chutes for back-yard miskins. In less than a decade, a new Birmingham had been born.

But there was another new Birmingham coming to life in these same years too. Such were the physical changes on the ground, as the Victorian city centre was carted away on the back of lorries, that it began to emerge almost unnoticed. You noticed it first if you lived out in Sparkbrook or Balsall Heath, or Aston or Handsworth. New faces began to appear – mostly men at first – with suitcases and a slip of paper, directing them to a bedsit in Victoria Terrace, or a villa in Albert Street. They came from Jamaica and Barbados, Bengal and Pakistan, looking for jobs in the foundries and workshops, at Lucas and Austin. They were bringing the Empire back home.

In the boom years of the 1950s, Birmingham had much need of a new workforce, and recruiting stations and travel bureaux were set up in the high streets of Bridgetown and Mirpur to entice them. The city needed bus conductors and nurses, car workers and electricians, and in the people came. Once they had found work, they sent photos - many of them taken by the Dyche studio - back to their families displaying all the symbols of a new status: a watch on each wrist, a newly starched uniform, a ballpoint in the top pocket.

Then, of course, the city began to agonise over what it should 'do' with its

new-found residents. Was it a matter of integration or separation, of zoning or dispersal? The reality, in fact, was that the new arrivals did what new arrivals had always done; they formed their own communities and networks, opened their shops and got on with it. Much as the Irish and Jews and Italians, the Quakers and Poles and Chinese, had done in the same streets in the years and the centuries before. But what was happening, even by the 1950s and long before the term was invented, was that Birmingham was becoming – had already become – an international city. The difference was that it had become international from within.

This, more than anything, was the missing element in Paul Cadbury's vision of 'the New Birmingham'.

But the destination these new settlers had headed for was changing even as they set foot off the bus. The place that had launched the steam-engine into the world and been the crossroads of the canals had become 'Motor City'. The Mini – the 'penny a mile car' – was its new flagship, and they rolled off the production line at Longbridge in ever-increasing numbers. And behind the Mini came the other icons of Birmingham's global market: BSA bikes, Lucas batteries, Typhoo Tea, Bird's Custard, Cadbury's Dairy Milk, HP Sauce. And behind all these were countless backstreet workshops, galvanising and electro-plating, welding and laminating, producing guns and gold rings, machine tools and moog synthesisers. The city of a thousand trades and a hundred thousand

Right *Ernest Dyche*, Studio Portrait, *c.1975*
Opposite *Ernest Dyche*, Studio Portraits, *c.1955*

products was in rude health. Was there a future in anything but manufacturing? Did there need to be?

The answer, as the 1960s unwound, was undoubtedly yes. The word from Whitehall was that Birmingham had simply become too successful and was growing too fast. Its jobs and its skills needed to be dispersed to more needy towns. To open a new factory in the city – second nature to generations of Birmingham workers – now required what they called an Industrial Development Certificate, and in most cases this request was refused. During the 1960s, something like 300 firms moved out of Birmingham, and took with them 80,000 jobs. For the first time in its history more people were moving out of Birmingham than moving in.

And the slide continued. By the mid-'80s some 200,000 jobs in manufacturing had gone. The lowest point in Birmingham's modern history was probably reached in 1985. By then many of the old industrial giants were history and local unemployment was pushing past 15 per cent. The city's headline band of the era – UB40 – took their name from the infamous unemployment card, and mixed Caribbean rhythms with white protest song sentiments when they sang:

I am a one in ten - a number on the list;
I am a one in ten, even though I don't exist...

In just about every way you could imagine – in planning, in employment and in vision – it was high time for another new Birmingham.

Great cities do not only dream; they act on their dreams. The transformation of Birmingham from this point onwards has been remarkable. The alchemy of that transformation is a complex one. It involved government money, European Regional Development funding and city council initiatives; but it also required the creativity and pride of the population of the city too.

More than anything, it meant connecting Birmingham once more with the people who lived in it. The Birmingham created in the Fifties and Sixties had been a masterpiece of urban engineering, with its concentric rings of roads, punctuated by underpasses. But it was hardly a city for people. The Inner Ring Road had solved the problem of congestion in the central streets, but it had squeezed the city centre like a greedy boa constrictor. Most people voted with their feet and kept well out of the way.

The new vision was hammered out in a series of meetings in Joseph Chamberlain's old house – a good place for dreaming – in March 1988. The Highbury Initiative laid out a blueprint for a city centre of interlocking squares, breaking through the concrete collar of the Ring Road, bringing pedestrians back to the surface, and expanding the city centre beyond its ancient (and entirely artificial) limits. For the first time since Joseph Chamberlain's vision of

Parisian boulevards Birmingham looked not to America for models of city living but to Europe. Subways and urban freeways were out; pedestrianised squares and public art were in.

The first obvious sign that the old order was changing was at the bottom of Broad Street, the area designated long ago for William Hayward's civic square. Between the library and the new International Convention Centre a Persian carpet of coloured bricks was rolled out. The traffic disappeared under the Hall of Memory, and people walked at ground level across the bridge to the new square. Centenary Square had art work and fountains and the first new city park for 50 years, but more importantly than any of these, it had people in it. They idled about; they sat on the benches and fed the pigeons, they watched the children playing in the fountain; they did nothing. These were the descendants of the Birmingham folk described by the French philosopher, Alexis De Toqueville, when he visited the town back in 1835:

These folk never have a minute to themselves. They work as if they must get rich by the evening and die they the next day. They are generally very intelligent people, but intelligent in the American way.

And here they were, doing nothing. Birmingham, for probably the first time in its history, was discovering leisure.

To walk across this square and beyond it is a journey backwards as well as forwards. The route begins beside the Hall of Memory, built mostly by Russian and Italian labour after the First World War. It passes Baskerville House, where John Baskerville hand-printed the books which 'astonished the librarians of Europe', and skirts the Birmingham Repertory Theatre, home to the oldest surviving repertory company in the land. It enters the Convention Centre, built on the site of the oldest purpose-built exhibition hall in the country, and past the doors to one of the world's greatest concert halls. The building of Symphony Hall fulfilled a promise made years before to the conductor of the City of Birmingham Symphony Orchestra, Sir Adrian Boult, for a concert hall to match the quality of his musicians. Its opening in 1991 announced Birmingham's arrival on the stage of great international cities.

And then, unexpectedly, the mall leads out onto a canal towpath and we have stepped back two centuries and more. The Birmingham Canal once brought the Black Country coal that fired the Industrial Revolution. Now its traffic moves at a more leisurely pace, bringing weekend bargees to Gas Street Basin, and tourists to the restaurants and cafes of Brindleyplace. Later the night shift will take over, and clubbers will noisily fill the bars and the night-clubs along Broad Street, and then drift away in the early hours, leaving the canal to its silent reflections.

Most large cities have a major river to carry their lives and history along; Birmingham carved its own waterway out of the sandstone ridge way back in

Left *Peter Williams*, PR Bhag Singh in the Ramgarhia Sikh Temple, Graham Street, in the old Jewellery Quarter *2001*
Opposite *Nick Hedges*, Two Birmingham families join the welcome for world leaders at the G8 Summit, Centenary Square *1998*

the 1760s. It was an early statement of intent by a place that wanted to make its own way in the world and to fashion its own destiny. The Birmingham Canal was perhaps the first dream of them all.

Where does this man-made waterway flow? In one direction the canal heads eastwards into Digbeth, where the factories of the old city still rattle with metal-working and blue railway arches tower over dark workshops. It still seems magical that metal this bright can come from workshops so dark. There are newer industries here too now, music studios that mix Asian bhangra and urban rap. This was once Birmingham's Ellis Island (though without the threat of being sent home), where the first generations of immigrants arrived by train and found cheap accommodation in the lodging-houses and courts of the surrounding streets. Now Digbeth is being transformed into the city's Learning Quarter. Soon the old railway terminus will have the new Library of Birmingham as its neighbour.

The canal leads north and west too, through Winson Green and Smethwick. Kids cycle and play along the towpath as they have done for 200 years, but now they come from Vietnam and China as well, from Bangladesh and the West Indies. There is a school here with no less than 19 different nationalities. The canal effortlessly threads its way through Asia and America and Europe.

And it heads south too, past expensive canalside apartments and private school playing fields, out to George Cadbury's 'factory in a garden' at Bournville, then to the University of Birmingham, and the Worcestershire countryside. Rich and poor, green and grey, grass and brick: Birmingham's contrasts have always been these.

More than anything, the Birmingham Canal is a symbol of a city replenishing itself. That renewal comes in different guises and different forms. It comes from reconnecting Birmingham with its past, but also drawing strength from the people who make up its future. And it comes from small things as well as big. All of these the post-war dreamers forgot.

There's no better place to see this process in action than in the city's Jewellery Quarter, where the old canal once terminated. The buildings here speak of an industry spanning 250 years, where a skilled craftsman could set up in business with little more than a gas-light and a handful of coins. From the beginning the Quarter attracted new settlers to the area, enticed by the chance to run their own business, to make it on their own two feet. This has always been one of the Birmingham dreams. The buildings remain, but the businesses are always changing. Many are now Asian-owned and producing jewellery for the city's Indian, Pakistani and Bangladeshi communities. Others have been converted to hi-tech industries, and the old church in St Paul's Square (where James Watt once worshipped) is now ringed by graphics studios and software companies. People have come back to live here too in loft apartments and studio flats. And the churches in the Quarter are changing too. Down in Graham Street what

was once Highbury Chapel was built by the Congregationalists 160 years ago. Later on it was taken over by the Methodists and then by the Baptists. Today it's a Sikh gurdwara.

This story could be repeated across the length and breadth of the city. In the back streets of Sparkbrook, in the bed-sits of Handsworth, in the high-rise flats of Newtown, a new generation is dreaming. As 'The Streets' put it:

The hazy fog over the Bull Ring;
The lazy way the birds sing;
A new baby is born every day...

How far has Birmingham come in these fifty years? It's been an extraordinary journey. From the 1950s and 1960s, when the city centre was lost in a frenzy of re-building. From the 1970s and 1980s, when much of the city's manufacturing was lost to relocation and recession. From the 1990s when Birmingham began to rediscover its past and its future.

Such is the physical geography of the place, but the changes in its human geography are more striking still. It's evident enough in the faces on New Street. This, despite its name, is one of the most ancient thoroughfares in the city, already old by Tudor times. But the name is right because the street is always new. The migrants who first wandered down it fifty years ago are now in their third generation, have settled down and spread throughout the city. Today the newest faces on New Street come from Somalia and Kosovo, from Iraq and Bosnia. You can find them at the top of New Street most days, where Joseph Chamberlain's Council House reminds the city that the first step to success is self-belief.

You can find them out at Cannon Hill Park too, speaking the international language of football to their new neighbours, or promenading – as their Victorian predecessors once did – between the flower-beds.

Soon they will no longer be new either, and another generation of settlers will be playing its part in the city's renewal. Birmingham draws on new arrivals, like the streams that still feed into its old canals. When the sculptor, Dhruva Mistry, designed the fountain and figures for Victoria Square he too drew on the metaphor of water. A quotation from T S Eliot's *Four Quartets* runs around the top pool, though most people are more likely to sit on it than read it. It could be the past. It could be the future. It could be Birmingham.

Dry the pool, dry concrete, brown edged,
And the pool was filled with water out of sunlight,
And the lotos rose, quietly, quietly,
The surface glittered out of heart of light,
And they were behind us, reflected in the pool.

The Photographs

Pete James

Head of Photographs, Birmingham Central Library

Birmingham's civic motto, 'Forward', embodies a vision of a city driven by the forces of change and progress. Over the last fifty or so years, Birmingham has undergone a remarkable transformation from an industrial to a post-industrial city. During the same period the city has also become home to one of the most culturally diverse populations in the UK. The process and effects of urban, social and cultural change in the city have provided photographers with a wealth of subject matter for documentary and creative projects. The photographs in this book represent but a small fraction of the work made by photographers in response to these changes.

The majority of the photographs published here are drawn from the extensive collections held by Birmingham Central Library. Over the last decade the Library has been pro-active in commissioning and acquiring such work in partnership with the photographers and with the support of a range of external agencies. The last two photo essays have been commissioned by the *be in Birmingham 2008* team to support the city's bid to be European Capital of Culture. These bodies of work will eventually be deposited in the Library's collections.

The photographers who made the images in this book share many of the aims of their 19th- and 20th-century predecessors in recording changes in Birmingham's human and physical landscape. However, as the variety of work reveals, they are not making simple records, they are making images that are stylistically individual, resulting in the production of documents that are not merely descriptive but subjective and allusive: an artistic response to the city.

These contemporary photographs now sit in the Library's collections alongside images by some of the greatest photographers of the 19th and 20th centuries: Roger Fenton, Francis Frith, Sir Benjamin Stone, Edweard Muybridge, Bill Brandt and Henri Cartier-Bresson. These collections, recently described by Colin Ford, former Director of the National Museum of Photography, Film and Television, as being 'world class' are at the centre of plans to create innovative cultural facilities and services in the new Library of Birmingham. The Library of Birmingham is itself at the heart of the city's bid to become capital of culture in 2008. The plans for the new library include dedicated facilities for its photography collections, with archival storage, increased public access to original material within the building via search rooms and dedicated exhibition spaces, and digital access beyond the institution.

The collective vision conveyed through these photographs is one of a city that is home to a wealth of creative photographic talent, and one whose regeneration, diversity and forward momentum inspires the creation of images that have a cultural significance far beyond the bounds of the city.

Matthew Murray, Heartlands People *1997*

Vanley Burke

The African-Caribbean Community in Birmingham **1970s – 2003**

Although it was not until the post-1945 period that an African-Caribbean presence of any size developed in the city, there is evidence of a black presence in Birmingham dating back to the 18th century. Birmingham's African-Caribbean community brought a new dimension to all aspects of life in the city including religion, politics, food and culture, where its impact is reflected in the Handsworth International Carnival, and the city's dance, theatre, poetry and music scene.

Jamaican-born photographer Vanley Burke has been living and working in Birmingham since 1965. He started to record the community around him in the late 1960s and has continued this personal journey to the present day. Burke's images represent a sensitive portrayal of black people and their presence in the city. His photographs not only focus on the cultural and collective aspects of the black community, but also on the more personal and quiet moments of people's daily existence. His understated photographs dispel myths and provide a rare and historically significant portrayal of his local community. Burke is currently documenting the Asian community and members of the Somali and Kurdish community who form part of the new generation of settlers in the city.

Vanley Burke's work has been published widely and shown in major exhibitions in Britain, Europe, America and South Africa. His photographs have also been used for the videos and record covers for the Birmingham-based band UB40.

Pupils from Grove Lane Junior School on a visit to the countryside *1981*

Vanley Burke   Schoolgirls, Soho House Museum, Handsworth *2003*   18

Children playing in Handsworth *1985*

Vanley Burke   Playing dominoes, Frighted Horse pub, Soho Road, Handsworth *1981*

Pool, Hockley *1980*

The Bar, Red Lion pub, Handsworth *1981*   23

Vanley Burke   Dance, Winson Green Community Centre *1981*

Football, Handsworth *1986*

Vanley Burke

Dr Roi Kwabena, Birmingham's Poet Laureate (2001-02)
at the Arts Fest, Centenary Square *2002*

Derek Bishton
and John Reardon

Home Front **1983 – 85**

The Handsworth area of Birmingham has become home to an ethnically and culturally diverse community of people that have come to live and work in the city. The area attracted intense media attention during the late 1970s and early 1980s, especially after the disturbances of 1981. Inevitably the issues which emerged nationally concentrated on crime and social unrest and portrayed Handsworth in a very negative way.

During the late 1970s, Derek Bishton and John Reardon were part of a collective of freelance photographers and graphic designers working for campaigning and community groups in the area. They were often asked by local groups to photograph specific events – protest meetings, anti-deportation campaigns, cultural occasions – and they thus became involved in the complex representation of a new and alternative history of the area. One of the key outcomes of this work was the exhibition and book *Home Front,* published in 1984. This sought to contextualise traditional documentary images dealing with the historical background to the black presence, racial stereotyping, industrial decline and different cultural heritages.

Derek Bishton worked on the editorial panel of *Ten:8* Magazine and now works as Editor of the *Electronic Telegraph*. John Reardon now works as a photographer for *The Observer*.

John Reardon, Eddie Chambers, artist *1980*

**Derek Bishton
and John Reardon**

John Reardon, Thornhill Road, outside the police station *1982*

Derek Bishton
and John Reardon   *John Reardon*, Muhammad Ali Centre, Handsworth *1983*

John Reardon, The langa at Smethwick gurdwara *1982*

John Reardon, Handsworth v Brixton, Handsworth Park *1983*

Derek Bishton, Prem Singh Raidi's clothing works, Handsworth *1983*   37

Left *John Reardon*, Sweet Memories; on the Soho Road,
Handsworth *1981*
Opposite *John Reardon*, Members of the Guru Nanak Nishkam
Sewak Jatha gurdwara, Handsworth *1983*

James O Davies, Peter Williams and Ian Leonard

Birmingham Jewellery Quarter **2000 – 2001**

Birmingham's Jewellery Quarter in Hockley contains the best and most extensive surviving group of Victorian and 20th-century buildings devoted to the manufacture of jewellery and similar goods in Europe. Some 6000 people are employed in the jewellery trade in the area including a significant number of jewellery firms run by and catering for members of the city's Indian, Pakistani and Bangladeshi communities. Regeneration initiatives such as the creation of the Museum of the Jewellery Quarter and the transformation of a former chapel on Graham Street into a Sikh temple have seen old properties given new economic and cultural life. The area is therefore a site of unique industrial archaeology, economic and cultural change, a visitor attraction and home to a diverse and thriving manufacturing community.

These photographs, taken by photographers working for English Heritage, were part of a joint project between Birmingham City Council and English Heritage to complete the most extensive architectural survey ever carried out in the Quarter. They were first published together with an exhibition held at the Birmingham School of Jewellery.

James O Davies's work has been published in two recent books, *Behind Bars: The Architectural History of English Prisons* and *Birmingham Jewellery Quarter, An Introduction and Guide*. Peter Williams joined English Heritage in 1975. Ian Leonard worked as a photographer for the British Museum and for English Heritage since 1993.

James O Davies, Gem Buildings, built in 1913 as a diamond cutting and polishing works *2000*

James O Davies,
Peter Williams
and Ian Leonard

James O Davies, A selection of jigs and dies in a workshop in the Jewellery Quarter, Hockley *2001*

James O Davies, The power press room in the workshops of No 94 Vyse Street, Hockley *2001*

**James O Davies,
Peter Williams
and Ian Leonard**

Peter Williams, Interior of the Rose Villa Tavern, Hockley *2001*

James O Davies,
Peter Williams
and Ian Leonard

Above *Peter Williams*, John Boot soldering a ring, Hockley *2001*
Opposite *Peter Williams*, a three seat jeweller's board or workbench, Hockley *2001*

46

James O Davies,
Peter Williams
and Ian Leonard

Above *Ian Leonard*, A cast-iron 19th century urinal in the Snowhill Viaduct, Livery Street *2001*
Opposite *James O Davies*, The Vaughton Gothic Works, Livery Street, a former badge, medal
and civic jewellery works of 1902

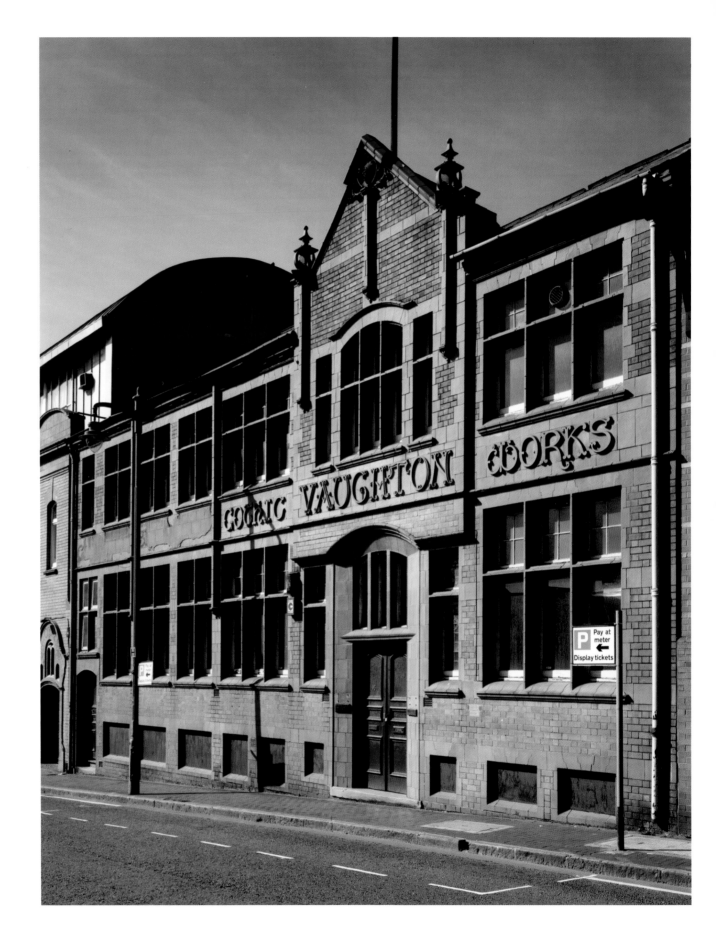

Above *Peter Williams*, Former premises of J & E Freeman, Icknield Street, Hockley *2001*

Opposite *James O Davies*, The former Newman Brothers coffin furniture factory,

Nos 13-15, Fleet Street, Hockley *2001*

Terry Lo

The Chinese Community in Birmingham **1970s – present day**

Birmingham is about as far away from the sea as you can get in England. This may explain why, unlike the port cities of Liverpool, London and Cardiff, it did not see large-scale Chinese migration until the 1960s. However, there were small numbers of Chinese people in the Birmingham area from at least the 1900s. Like many of the migrant communities in the West Midlands, the present structure of the Chinese population took shape in the 1950s and 1960s. The expanding post-war economy, changing family structures and food tastes created a demand for convenience food, and Chinese catering businesses spread throughout the land. The consolidation of Birmingham's Chinese population – estimated at just over 5,000 in the 2001 population Census – is reflected in the development of the Chinatown area in the Arcadian Centre. This has become the setting for the annual Chinese New Year celebrations.

Terry Lo was born in Hong Kong. He studied photography at Wolverhampton Polytechnic where he made this body of work as part of his final-year project. Lo's photographs reveal the ways in which Birmingham's Chinese community strive to preserve their own cultural traditions whilst also integrating with those of their home city. The work was exhibited at the Midlands Arts Centre and in Birmingham Central Library.

Terry Lo   Conkers *1993*   54

Mother-tongue language class, Chinese Community Centre *1993*

Terry Lo   Tai Chi class, Chinese Community Centre *1993*

Terry Lo   Teacher and pupil, Westminster Junior School, Handsworth *1993*   58

Mr Yim and family *1993*

Tom Merilion

Moseley Road Baths **1997**

During the Victorian and Edwardian era, Birmingham's city fathers created a citywide network of public baths and swimming pools to encourage better personal hygiene and physical recreation amongst the 'working classes'. Built in the Gothic Renaissance style, Moseley Road Baths opened in Balsall Heath in 1907. As well as providing facilities for washing and swimming, the pool area was also covered and used for dances.

In 1989 Tom Merilion, then a final-year student of Media Production at Newcastle Polytechnic, was commissioned to make a short film for the BBC2 series 10 X 10. Merilion chose his local swimming pool, Moseley Road Baths, or perhaps more correctly the communities and characters who use the bath's facilities, as the subject for his film.

Almost ten years later, Merilion began to make still images at the baths, which were then threatened with closure. Merilion captured the diversity of communities and of people young and old who use the baths, and the wide range of activities, from baptisms to mother and toddler groups that take place there. This self-initiated project led to a partnership with Birmingham Central Library resulting in an exhibition at Midlands Arts Centre in 1998 and the subsequent acquisition of his work for the Library's collections. Merilion's colour portrait of 'Richard and Gillian' was selected for the John Kobal Portrait Award exhibition in 1999.

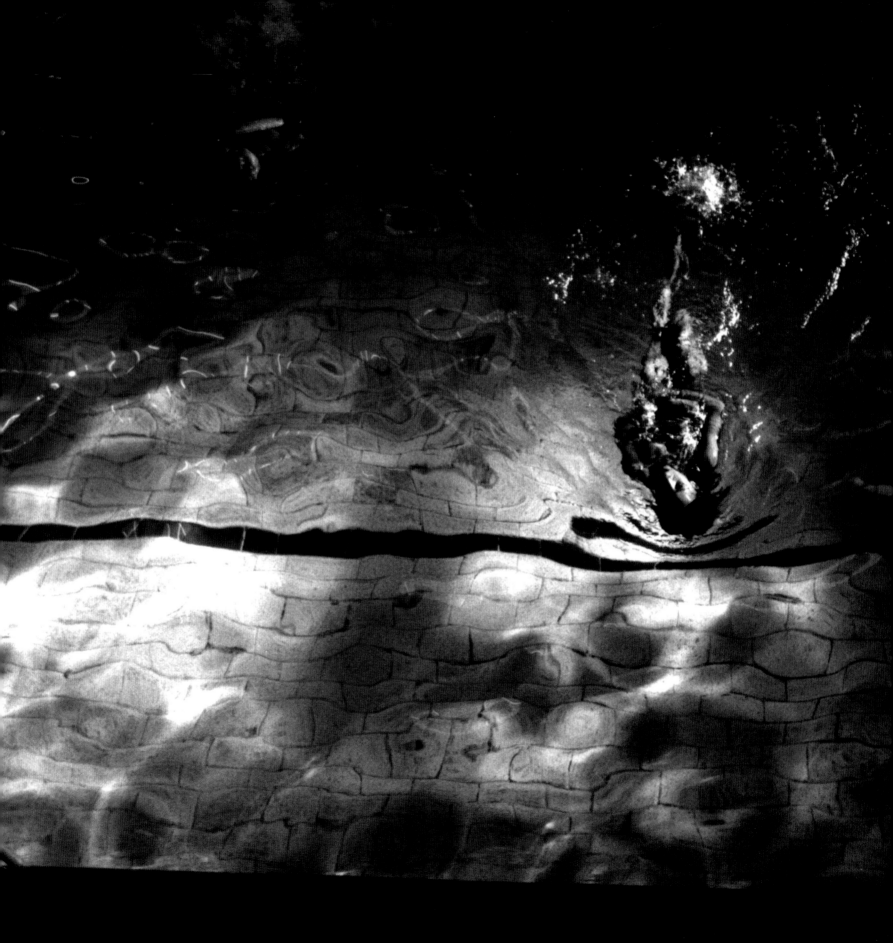

Tom Merilion   Moseley Road Baths

Tom Merilion   Moseley Road Baths

Tom Merilion   Moseley Road Baths

Susan Green

Birmingham (formerly Handsworth) International Carnival **1993 – 2000**

Celebrating carnival in the Caribbean dates back to the 18th century when Birmingham's major connection with the region was manifested through the production of guns and chains for the slave trade. Today carnival is celebrated in many cities throughout the world.

Birmingham's first Carnival was staged in September 1984. Over a two-day period it attracted some 30,000 revellers. Today the event has grown to become a major event rivalling those held in Notting Hill and Leeds. Carnival now attracts participants and spectators from all over the city for the two days, the Saturday being designated as children's carnival day.

Handsworth resident and photographer Susan Green has recorded Birmingham (formerly Handsworth) International Carnival for the last ten years. Her images capture the design and construction of costumes by local troupes, the parade of masqueraders, and the MAS Bands, Steel bands and drummers that perform there.

Originally from the North-East, Susan Green moved to Birmingham to set up the city's first photography gallery, The Triangle Gallery. She has worked as a photographer, as an editor of *Ten:8* Magazine, and as an advisor to a range of photography and arts organisations in the UK.

Trainers and shoes decorated for Carnival, Oakland Centre Carnival Troupe, Handsworth *1993*

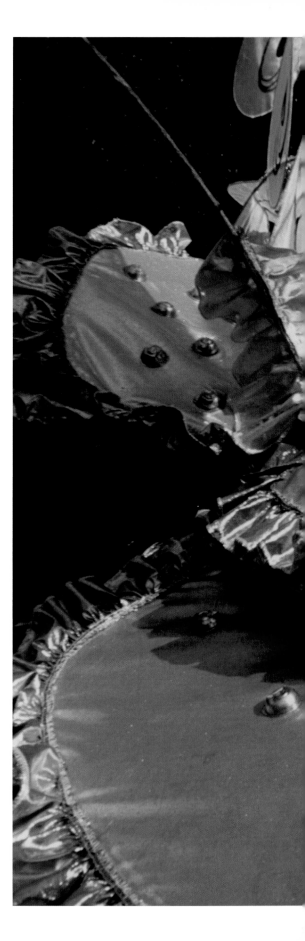

Susan Green

Above Handsworth Carnival *1993*

Right Handsworth Carnival *1993*

Susan Green   Handsworth Carnival *1993*

Oakland Centre Carnival Troupe *2000*

Susan Green   Oakland Centre Carnival Troupe *2000*

Handsworth Carnival *1993*

Willoughby Gullachsen

Hidden Birmingham **1995**

Willoughby Gullachsen has worked as a press photographer in Birmingham for over 40 years. During that time he gained privileged access to people and places, enabling him to discover aspects of the city rarely seen by people in their everyday lives: a hidden Birmingham.

In 1996, Gullachsen set out to capture and reveal some of these hidden histories with his camera. He secured images above and below the surface of the city and behind the walls and doors of institutions that do not ordinarily provide public access. His 'behind the scenes' views of seemingly familiar public places and spaces opened the eyes of many local people who thought they already knew their city well.

Following service as an RAF photographer in South Africa, India, Iran and Iraq, Willoughby 'Gus' Gullachsen established a successful career as a freelance photographer working for regional and national publications, television companies including ABC, ATV and the BBC, and theatres such as the Birmingham Rep. He is the father of Lorentz Gullachsen whose work also appears in this book.

Opposite Bishop's chair, St Philip's Cathedral, Colmore Row *1995*
Following pages, left Preserved façade, Corporation Street *1995*
Following pages, right St Lazar Serbian Orthodox Church, Bournville *1995*

Above Old Jewish cemetery, Edgbaston *1995*

Previous pages, left Portrait of Cardinal Newman, The Library, The Oratory, Hagley Road *1995*

Willoughby Gullachsen   **Previous pages, right** Birmingham Gun Barrel Proof House, Digbeth *1995*

The Rock Face, Aston *1995*

Dave Ruffles

Birmingham Allotments **1993 – 96**

At a time when some allotments in Britain have become neglected and disused, those in Birmingham prove there is new life in an old tradition. Many of the city's allotment sites were established as part of the 'Dig for Victory' campaign in the Second World War. In the post-war period, new citizens from India, Pakistan, the Caribbean, Ireland and elsewhere in Europe who have made their homes in Birmingham, brought with them the tradition of home-grown food. The use of allotments in the city now involves people of different ages, personalities and cultures, creating a real sense of community through their individual and collective efforts.

Dave Ruffles began photographing allotments in his native city as part of his Master of Arts studies at the University of Central England in 1996. He became fascinated by the architecture in these urban gardens: an architecture that varied from small tool lockers to brick-built sheds with their own fireplaces, some of which virtually served as a second home. He was also struck by the way in which the allotment holders gave new life to scrap materials: old tyres and wheels became plant pots and old engine parts were strung up to act as audible scarecrows to deter birds from stealing seeds and damaging crops. Ruffles's images reflect the strong sense of community found amongst the holders of these inner-city gardens and the way in which they serve as an oasis of tranquillity for plant, animal and human life in the centre of a bustling city.

Dave Ruffles worked as a scientific photographer at the University of Birmingham before recently moving to Ireland. His work has been shown at the Midlands Arts Centre and Birmingham Museum and Art Gallery.

Dave Ruffles   Birmingham Allotments

Ravi Deepres

Capitalising on Culture and other commissions **2002 – 03**

In any city that, like Birmingham, is home to so many different nationalities, issues of identity, culture and place will always be a subject of interest to photographers. Ravi Deepres has explored and reflected these issues in two recent projects. Although both draw on the city and supporters from its local football clubs for subject matter, the projects themselves are very distinct.

The first, Patriots, is a personal exploration of national, social and individual identity through observation of the dynamics and iconography of football supporters. In Patriots, Deepres photographs individuals and massed crowds to illustrate the assumption and performance of shared identities, which in turn reflect the fluidity of modern-day influences of (multi) cultural, national and international society.

The second, Capitalising on Culture, is a commercial commission to create images representing youth culture and ethnic diversity in the city. The resulting images have been used in an advertising campaign organised by Birmingham Arts Marketing to support Birmingham's bid for Capital of Culture.

Over recent years, Ravi Deepres has established an international reputation for his photography and video work. His video and photographic collaborations with Japanese choreographer Saburo Teshigawara have been seen at the Edinburgh Festival and at theatres and festivals around the world. Apart from commercial work in dance and fashion, his photographic works have been exhibited in shows across the UK.

Top Bluenose baby, Capitalising on Culture commission
Above Baggies fans, Capitalising on Culture commission

England Supporters, Capitalising on Culture commission

Opposite Girls (laughing into their hands), Capitalising on Culture commission
Above Asian England Supporters face painting, Patriots series

Ravi Deepres   In the Park, Cricket and Cultural Identity series

Claire Richardson

Surviving Industries in Birmingham **1997**

During the 19th century Birmingham's reputation as an industrial and manufacturing centre led to it being described as the 'city of a thousand trades'. It established a world-wide reputation for the quality and diversity of products – from buttons to ship's anchors – made in its workshops and foundries. Although Birmingham is now moving into a post-industrial era with an economy increasingly dominated by the financial, service and tourist industries, many manufacturing firms still operate in the city. Some of these have been in business in Birmingham for over a century.

In a self-initiated project undertaken whilst a photography student at Sandwell College, Claire Richardson set out to research and record eight such companies: Halladay's Drop Forgings; IMI Birmingham Mint; T I Reynolds; Bishton's Silversmiths; B Mason & Sons; Francis B Wilmott; Westley Richards, and Rainsford & Lynes. Some have maintained working practices rooted in the 19th century whilst others have introduced new machinery, thereby allowing women to become employed in areas previously the exclusive domain of male workers.

Claire Richardson now works as a photographer at the National Museum of Science and Industry in London.

Claire Richardson   TI Reynolds Rings *1997*

IMI Birmingham Mint *1997*

Claire Richardson

Above IMI Birmingham Mint *1997*

Opposite Halladay's Drop Forgings *1997*

Claire Richardson   IMI Birmingham Mint *1997*

Halladay's Drop Forgings *1997*

Matthew Murray

Heartlands People **1997**

Matthew Murray's intimate portrait of the everyday lives of people in Nechells began life as a self-initiated project undertaken whilst a final-year MA Visual Communications student at the University of Central England. The resulting exhibition was made possible through the partnership of Birmingham Central Library and the Birmingham Heartlands Development Corporation.

Murray cast his camera towards the residents of Nechells, an inner-city area of Birmingham at a time of dramatic change in the locality. Regenerative initiatives undertaken by the Heartlands Development Corporation included the building of business parks and the creation of Britain's first new urban village. Whereas other similar projects have focussed on the difficulties of inner-city life and poorly conceived development plans, Murray's light and hopeful study concentrated on uncovering the warmth, humour and personality of the people these changes affected most: the local residents.

Matthew Murray now works as a commercial photographer. His images have been published in *The Observer* Magazine, *Vanity Fair*, *Cosmopolitan* and *ID* Magazine amongst others.

Matthew Murray   Heartlands People *1997*

Matthew Murray   Heartlands People *1997*

Matthew Murray   Heartlands People *1997*

Nick Hedges

Conurbation **1998 – 2002**

These Birmingham photographs are part of a larger, ongoing project by one of the region's leading documentary photographers, Nick Hedges. The project seeks to illustrate a contemporary response to the post-war planning initiative Conurbation, published originally in 1948. The project is being undertaken by a consortium led by the Centre for Urban and Regional Studies at the University of Birmingham that includes Birmingham Central Library, the Bournville Village Trust, and the University of Wolverhampton.

Nick Hedges's project revisits both the realities of the West Midlands conurbation as seen in 1948, and reviews the planners' visions for the conurbation 50 years on. He began by using some of the themes and many images that formed the original publication as a point of departure. However, rather than producing new work that was simply responsive to the past, Hedges considered it important to acknowledge the changing priorities for city communities in the 21st century. He therefore turned his camera to recording the changing nature of work and employment; the vital contributions that multi-ethnic communities make to our lives and culture, and a redefinition of leisure to include the culture of shopping. These images reflect some of those concerns.

Nick Hedges studied photography at Birmingham School of Art before going on to work as a freelance photographer undertaking commissions for MENCAP, CSV, the Royal Town Planning Institute and Penguin Books. He completed a two-year documentation of factory work in the Midlands, published as *Born to Work*, in 1982. He has most recently been working as subject leader in photography at the University of Wolverhampton.

A Birmingham policeman contributes to the security arrangements for the G8 summit, Broad Street *1998*

Nick Hedges

Street conversation between senior citizens making use of the newly pedestrianised
section of New Street *1998*

Mother and daughter relax by the 'Floozy in the Jaccuzzi',
outside Birmingham Council House *1998*

Above Rollerblade skaters enjoying a summer's day in the pedestrianised section of New Street *1998*
Opposite Young man relaxing in Centenary Square during his lunch hour *1998*

Luke Unsworth

The Bull Ring **1999 – 2001**

Luke Unsworth first started photographing cities whilst studying photography at Stockport. He became interested in trying to represent the secrets a city can express when the normally busy streets are quiet and empty. Since moving to Birmingham, Unsworth's fascination for photographing cities has deepened, along with an interest in photographing the people who inhabit these urban spaces.

The building of the new Bull Ring, the largest city-centre retail-led development project in Europe, itself part of a major project to regenerate over 40 acres of land in the centre of Birmingham, proved an ideal place for Unsworth to develop his photographic interests. Starting in 1999 before any of the redevelopment commenced, Unsworth photographed St Martin's market and the Bull Ring Centre, all of which have now been demolished. Unsworth continued to record these changes supported by funding from the Birmingham Alliance, Eastside and Birmingham Central Library. He has now extensively photographed the demolition process of the entire Bull Ring area, often taking pictures inside buildings shortly before they came down.

Luke Unsworth has worked for various local bodies including Millennium Point, Birmingham Central Library, Carlton Television and Eastside. Most recently Unsworth photographed 'Shadow Games', an art project created to mark the opening of the World Indoor Athletics Championships in Birmingham.

Luke Unsworth   Bell Street Subway, 2 July 1999   132

Subway, St Martin's Market, 26 June 1999

Luke Unsworth

Stairs to the roof of the old trolley car park,
Bull Ring Centre, 8 January 2000

Luke Unsworth   Window cleaners climbing The Rotunda, 1 July 2000

Fire buckets in the old trolley car park, Bull Ring Centre, 8 January 2000

Nicola Gotts

Cultural Events at the Arcadian Centre **2000**

By 2012, Birmingham will be the first British city to have a minority white population. It is currently home to people of 88 different nationalities and the city is discovering how different ethnic communities can live, work and have fun together. One of the best demonstrations of the way in which people from these different nationalities are coming together is witnessed in the diversity of audiences in the celebration of cultural festivities such as the St Patrick's Day Parade, Vaishki, Diwali and the Mega Mela.

For several years the Arcadian Centre, situated in the city's Chinese Quarter, has played host to two such events, Birmingham's celebrations for Chinese New Year and the Latin American Festival. The Chinese New Year celebrations include traditional lion dances, acrobats and the Pak Ming Opera group. The Latin American festival, the most established festival of its kind in the UK includes Salsa/Merengue dancers, Brazilian samba dancers, and folklore and flamenco groups.

Nicola Gotts studied photography at Newcastle College of Art and Design. She is now a freelance photographer living and working in Birmingham.

Nicola Gotts   Chinese New Year, Arcadian Centre *2000*

Chinese New Year, Arcadian Centre *2000*

Nicola Gotts Latin American Festival, Arcadian Centre *2000*

Latin American Festival, Arcadian Centre *2000*

John Davies

Metropoli **2000**

John Davies is one of Britain's most outstanding photographers whose international reputation has grown steadily in the field of landscape photography. Davies recently completed a project to photograph the major industrial and post-industrial cities of Britain. He called this project 'Metropoli'.

Birmingham Central Library supported Davies's project by establishing a commission to photograph the city. Here, as with earlier work, Davies's chosen point of view was often from an elevated vantage point, giving him a wide skyline and allowing him to record the multi-layered landscape of the city.

His project includes photographs of Symphony Hall, the International Convention Centre, the Hyatt Hotel, the Sea Life Centre and Brindleyplace, developments that all stand on land formerly occupied by industrial and commercial premises. These now serve as ample testament to the city's changing role from an industrial city to one whose economy is driven by culture, business, visitor attractions and service industries. He also reveals the ways in which the newly created public spaces of Centenary Square and Victoria Square, and those alongside the canal in Brindleyplace, all linked by paved pedestrian walkways, have taken over from roads to form the new heart and arteries of the city centre.

Chamberlain Square *2000*

John Davies

Above Mass House Circus Queensway 2000

Above right Brindleyplace 2000

Above New Street Station *2000*
Above right Centenary Square *2000*

John Davies Brindleyplace *2000*

Brindleyplace *2000*

Tim Smith

Birmingham's Sikh and Muslim Community **2001**

For the past twenty years, Tim Smith has been photographing many of the cosmopolitan communities which now play such an important role in British towns and cities. These pictures are part of a long-term project exploring the lives of several generations of people with roots in India, Pakistan, Bangladesh and Sri Lanka. Photographs taken all over the country explore how a small number of pioneer settlers have grown into a rich mix of established communities, numbering close to two million people.

The diversity of British Asian communities is reflected in Birmingham itself, where different cultures, religions and languages from the Indian sub-continent have made themselves part of the fabric of the city. These pictures were taken in and around some of the most visible landmarks of the Muslim and Sikh presence, the mosques and gurdwaras that punctuate Birmingham's skyline. As well as their role as places of worship they act as important social centres, and provide a wide range of services to the communities they serve.

Tim Smith is a freelance photographer based in Yorkshire. He is currently working for several editorial and commercial clients, arts organisations, and on a number of long-term exhibition and book projects. He set up and runs the photographic department of the Bradford Heritage Recording Unit, part of Bradford Art Galleries and Museums. His work has been published in *The Guardian*, *The Observer*, *The Independent*, *The Times* and the *Times Educational Supplement*.

Cleaning the Sikh symbol, the Khanda, during celebrations marking Guru Gobind Singh's birthday
at the Ramgarhia Sikh Temple on Graham Street

Tim Smith

Musicians passing Birmingham's largest gurdwara in Handsworth during the festival of Baisakhi, marking the Sikh New Year

An Islamic funeral service at the Central Jamia Mosque Ghamkol Sharif in Small Heath

Right Preparing for prayers at the Central Jamia Mosque on Golden Hillock Road in Small Heath

Opposite Women cleaning the Sikh flag during celebrations marking Guru Gobind Singh's birthday at the Ramgarhia Sikh Temple on Graham Street

Staircase to the main prayer hall in the Central Jamia Mosque

Michael Hallett

Birmingham Constructed Panoramas **2001 – 2003**

The conventional camera has a limited field of view. From the earliest days photographers sought to expand this restricted field of vision by creating panoramic images. The two most common methods were to make a succession of overlapping negatives and then paste together a corresponding sequence of prints, to use a rotating camera with moving plates or films or simply to use a camera with a wide-angle lens. Examples of historic images produced by each of these methods can be found in the Library's collections.

Although Hallett's images share their format with their predecessors, they use significantly different technology and expand upon what has gone before. The images captured using both conventional and digital cameras are transformed into panoramic constructions using a design software package; the images are then produced by an ink jet printer. The past and the present are freely intermixed, expanding both the content and the time represented in the completed image.

Michael Hallett, former Principal Lecturer at the School of Theoretical and Historical Studies at the University of Central England, now works as a freelance photographer and writer. He is currently working with the Birmingham Alliance and the Central Library on a book and exhibition of photographs about the Bull Ring.

The Bull Ring development showing the retaining wall *27 July 2001*

Michael Hallett   Victoria Square, 30 January 2003

Text inscribed on fountain: AND THE POOL WAS FILLED WITH WATER

Michael Hallett   Chamberlain Square, Town Hall and Central Library *23 & 25 January 2003*

From the Rotunda to St Martin in the Bull Ring Church. The Bullring *20 February 2003*

Lorentz Gullachsen

Movers and Shakers **2001 –**

In 1986 Birmingham City Council commissioned Lorentz Gullachsen to make a series of images for an advertising campaign promoting the city of Birmingham in the national press and on poster sites. He was also commissioned to produce photographs to promote Birmingham's bid to host the Olympic Games. Gullachsen was therefore at the forefront of efforts to create new images representing the post-industrial Birmingham that was emerging towards the end of the last century.

Early in 2001, Lorentz Gullachsen decided to initiate a personal project to be undertaken alongside his commercial work. His aim is to make a series of environmental portraits of the people, some famous, some less well known, who are helping Birmingham become a dynamic international city for the 21st century. The subjects are drawn from all fields of endeavour including business, culture, sport and education. Gullachsen brings his extensive knowledge of commercial portrait photography to the project, the results of which will be shown in the new Bull Ring in February 2004.

Lorentz Gullachsen trained at the Birmingham School of Photography before going on to build an international career as a commercial location photographer specialising in automotive, landscape and portrait work.

Dennis Amiss, Chief Executive, Warwickshire County Cricket Club *2001*

Lorentz Gullachsen   Karen Brady, Managing Director, Birmingham City Football Club *2001*

David Bintley, Artistic Director, Birmingham Royal Ballet *2001*

Lorentz Gullachsen   Doug Ellis, Chairman, Aston Villa Football Club *2001*

John Towers, Chairman MG-Rover Group *2001*

Tom Merilion

Birmingham: New Perspectives **1999 – 2003**

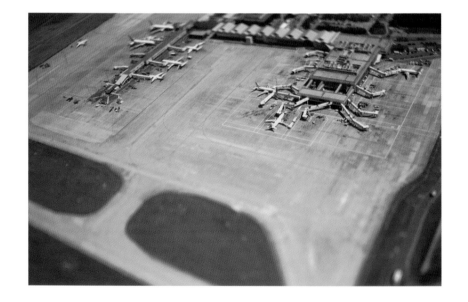

These extraordinary images are the result of two commissions. The first occurred in 1999 when Birmingham Library commissioned Tom Merilion to make a body of work for an exhibition entitled 'Concrete Dreams'. Over an 18-month period, Merilion perfected a technique that enabled him to evoke the visual feel of the planner's models from which many key Birmingham buildings of the 1970s evolved. This unique perspective allowed viewers to question accepted notions of scale, planning, aesthetics, architecture and beauty. The photographs offered the viewer an opportunity to take the role of planner and re-arrange the blocks once again to create their own concrete dream of Birmingham.

The second commission came in 2002 when the *be in Birmingham 2008* team commissioned further images of Birmingham and the West Midlands for the exhibition and book *The People and the City, A Cultural Portrait of Birmingham*. Once again Merilion produced a series of images imbued with affection for, and familiarity with, the structures of the city. These images are a powerful memento of the city in which Merilion spent his youth. They now offer a new perspective on Birmingham to people beyond the city.

Tom Merilion is a film-maker and photographer. His work has been shown in Birmingham, London and Belfast and published in *DPICT*, *The Architectural Review* and *The Independent on Sunday* Magazine.

Tom Merilion   University of Birmingham *2003*

Top right Longbridge *2000*
Above right Spaghetti Junction *2000*

Tom Merilion   Walkway, Centenary Square *2000*

Alpha Tower *2000*

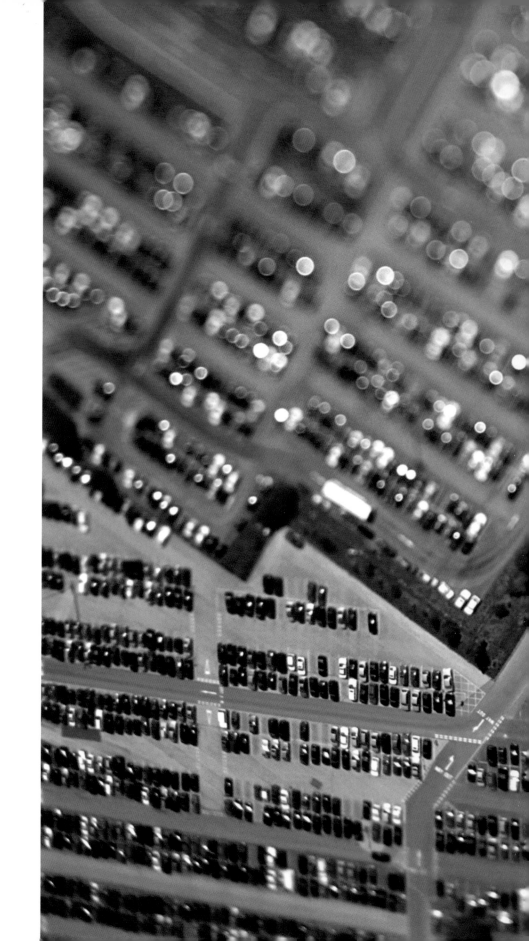

Tom Merilion   National Exhibition Centre Car Park *2000*

Tom Merilion   Birmingham Central Mosque *2000*

New Street Station *2000*

Brian Griffin

Birmingham: a Cultural Portrait **2003**

Brian Griffin's distinctive style of portraiture defined the look and feel of the 1980s and early 1990s. So much so that in 1989 The Guardian described him as 'Photographer of the Decade'. Having published a series of acclaimed portraits in his books *Power* (1984) and *Work* (1989), Griffin left the world of photography and went into making films and commercials. He returned to Birmingham in 2003 having been commissioned by the Capital of Culture bid team to create a new series of portraits of some of the people – planners, writers, couriers, image makers, artists – who make modern Birmingham tick.

Griffin began by photographing the statue of the Lunar Men, Matthew Boulton, James Watt and William Murdoch, whose ability to make extraordinary things happen is still alive and well in the city today. He went on to make 37 portraits in two weeks, sometimes of people well known, but often of those who work behind the scenes and without the public recognition they deserve. Griffin has controlled the elements and worked closely with his subjects to produce a series of portraits that shed new light on the city and the people who make it what it is today, and what it will become tomorrow.

Brian Griffin studied photography at Manchester Polytechnic School of Photography. Since graduating he has established his own studio, and shown and published work around the world. He now makes films and commercials.

Ashia Hansen, triple jumper, with Peter and Theresa Horte, at Two Towers *2003*

Above Ravi Deepres, photographer, and Sandra Hall, performer *2003*
Opposite Vanley Burke, photographer *2003*
Following pages, left Hellen Fitzgerald, cellist, in the kitchen at the Council House *2003*
Following pages, right Ava Ming and Nylah Ahmed, writers *2003*

Brian Griffin

Above Benny Gray, Director, Space Organisation, at the Custard Factory *2003*
Opposite Fuzz Townsend, musician, with Honor and Oscar, at Millennium Point *2003*

Above The Lunar Men, Broad Street *2003*
Opposite Dean Cargill, courier, at The Mailbox *2003*

This book has been commissioned by:

be in Birmingham 2008
A EUROPEAN CAPITAL OF CULTURE

With funds from:

Advantage
West Midlands

Birmingham City Council

A Sears Pocknell Book

Editorial Direction	Roger Sears
Art Direction	David Pocknell
Editor	Michael Leitch
Designer	Jon Allan, Pocknell Studio
Artwork and typesetting	Harry Pocknell, Pocknell Studio

Copyright © Birmingham City Council, 2003
Published by Birmingham Library Services

ISBN 0 7093 02436

A CIP catalogue record for this book is available from the British Library

This book is sold subject to the condition that it shall not, by way of trade or otherwise, be lent,
re-sold, hired out or otherwise circulated without the publisher's consent in any form of cover or
binding other than that in which it is published and without a similar condition being imposed on
the subsequent purchaser.

All rights reserved. No part of this book may be reproduced or utilised in any form or by any means,
electronic or mechanical, including photocopying, recording or by any information storage and retrieval
system, without permission in writing from the publisher.

Printed by Imago Publishing Ltd, in Spain